# CLINT EASTWOOD

## The Illustrated Biography

### BY RICHARD SCHICKEL
### AND THE EDITORS OF LIFE

## TIME HOME ENTERTAINMENT

**President**  Richard Fraiman

**Vice President, Business Development & Strategy**
Steven Sandonato

**Executive Director, Marketing Services**
Carol Pittard

**Executive Director, Retail & Special Sales**
Tom Mifsud

**Executive Publishing Director**  Joy Butts

**Director, Bookazine Development & Marketing**
Laura Adam

**Finance Director**  Glenn Buonocore

**Associate Publishing Director**  Megan Pearlman

**Assistant General Counsel**  Helen Wan

**Assistant Director, Special Sales**  Ilene Schreider

**Book Production Manager**  Suzanne Janso

**Design & Prepress Manager**
Anne-Michelle Gallero

**Brand Manager**  Roshni Patel

**Associate Prepress Manager**  Alex Voznesenskiy

**Assistant Brand Manager**  Stephanie Braga

**Special thanks:** Christine Austin, Katherine Barnet, Jeremy Biloon, Jim Childs, Susan Chodakiewicz, Rose Cirrincione, Lauren Hall Clark, Jacqueline Fitzgerald, Christine Font, Jenna Goldberg, Hillary Hirsch, David Kahn, Amy Mangus, Robert Marasco, Kimberly Marshall, Amy Migliaccio, Nina Mistry, Dave Rozzelle, Adriana Tierno, Vanessa Wu

ISBN 10: 1-61893-034-6
ISBN 13: 978-1-61893-034-7
Library of Congress Control Number: 2012940781

"LIFE" is a registered trademark of Time Inc.

We welcome your comments and suggestions about LIFE Books. Please write to us at:
LIFE Books, Attention: Book Editors
PO Box 11016, Des Moines, IA 50336-1016

If you would like to order any of our hardcover Collector's Edition books, please call us at 1-800-327-6388. (Monday through Friday, 7 a.m.—8 p.m., or Saturday, 7 a.m.—6 p.m. Central Time).

## LIFE ICONS

**Managing Editor**  Robert Sullivan

**Director of Photography**
Barbara Baker Burrows

**Creative Director**  Anke Stohlmann

**Deputy Picture Editor**  Christina Lieberman

**Special Contributing Writer**  Richard Schickel

**Writer-Reporter**  Amy Lennard Goehner

**Copy Editors**  Parlan McGaw (Chief),
Barbara Gogan

**Photo Associate**  Sarah Cates

**Consulting Picture Editors**  Mimi Murphy (Rome), Tala Skari (Paris)

**Editorial Director**  Stephen Koepp

**Editorial Operations Director**
Michael Q. Bullerdick

### EDITORIAL OPERATIONS

Richard K. Prue (Director), Brian Fellows (Manager), Richard Shaffer (Production), Keith Aurelio, Charlotte Coco, Tracey Eure, Kevin Hart, Mert Kerimoglu, Rosalie Khan, Patricia Koh, Marco Lau, Brian Mai, Po Fung Ng, Rudi Papiri, Robert Pizaro, Barry Pribula, Clara Renauro, Katy Saunders, Hia Tan, Vaune Trachtman

**Endpapers** Clint Eastwood's handprints in the sidewalk at Gruman's Chinese Theater in Los Angeles. *George Rose/Getty*

**Page 1** The star in Carmel, California, where he lives, in 2000. *Ken Regan/Camera 5*

**Pages 2–3** In 1982, by the sea in Carmel. *Ken Regan/Camera 5*

**These pages** At the 2003 Cannes Film Festival. *Emanuele Scorcelletti/Contrasto/Redux*

# CLINT EASTWOOD

## The Illustrated Biography

# WHAT
## Makes an
# ICON?

That's a hard question to answer. To paraphrase the late Supreme Court justice Potter Stewart: You know one when you see one.

Some things help. A visage on Mount Rushmore is a confirmer, certainly. A "lifetime achievement award" bestowed by a respected organization—cultural, political, institutional—is often indicative. It used to be: The cover of LIFE magazine sometimes pointed to iconic status. Oh, not when it was given over to the latest 20-year-old starlet or supermodel, but when it pictured a person of deep accomplishment, a person with a track record of success who walked forth each day with the esteem of his or her peers and the admiration of the public. "Did you see who's on the cover of the latest LIFE?" That person may have just been anointed an icon by society at large, or might be well on the way.

The question itself—What makes an icon?—is permeated by je ne sais quoi. What *is* an icon? Must

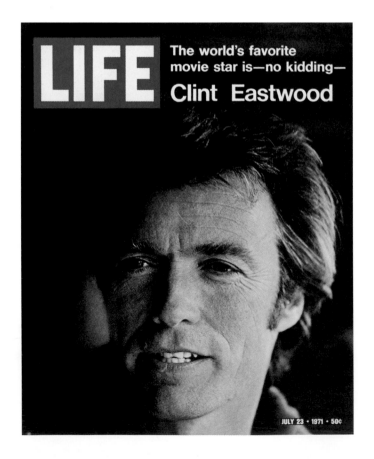

LIFE
The world's favorite movie star is—no kidding—
Clint Eastwood

JULY 23 · 1971 · 50¢

it be a hero? Must one be older? Do there exist, shall we say, borderline icons? Are there any who are inarguably, irrefutably icons?

These are questions we asked ourselves at LIFE Books when we decided to start this new line of commemoratives: illustrated biographies that would be focused tightly on the lives of the giants among us, each volume attempting to show—in words and pictures (many photographs never seen or long forgotten; some photographs famous and, well, iconic)—what the winding road was like for these extraordinary people. If LIFE was to get back in the icon-making game in earnest, we wanted to get it right.

We certainly wanted to launch with the right first choice. Very quickly, a nomination was made: "Clint."

"Well, that's probably part of it," one of us said. "You might be an icon if you don't need a second name."

Indeed, while there are many other Clintons or Clints, there are no other "Clints"—certainly not in America, perhaps not in the world. The closer we looked at his life, which we had visited many times before in LIFE's pages, the more sure we became that he was the correct choice. He was the epitome of the Hollywood hero, but he always went his own way, outside of (if not at odds with) Tinseltown. He stretched himself, both within and outside of his movie career, even serving a term as his town's mayor. He had enjoyed, to boot, one of those fanzine-friendly personal lives that fascinate. (Was Liz Taylor an icon? You bet. And she was the whole package.)

Clint seemed a fine choice, and we realized quickly that we had advantages in telling his tale. One of our old friends, veteran *Time* magazine film critic Richard Schickel, had not only written on and made film documentaries about Clint in the past, but had contributed to LIFE Books previously. We phoned Richard, and his detailed appraisal of Clint's career provides the narrative of the book you hold in your hands. Then too, others at LIFE had dropped in on Clint a few times through the years—in Carmel or on the set—and so we already had his evolving feelings during his journey to icon-hood. All of Clint's

KELLI ULDALL/CARMEL MAGAZINE

**OPPOSITE:** In 1971, the film *Dirty Harry* was about to kick-start Clint's climb to iconic status. LIFE granted him the cover but expressed some skepticism in the copy. We are skeptical no more. Clint, above at home with wife Dina in Carmel, California, wasn't worried by naysayers back when and isn't concerned about whatever he's called today. We call him: an icon.

quotations in the Schickel text are direct to Richard, of course, and everything that Clint says in the picture captions was, unless otherwise noted, direct to us as well.

And so with Clint we start our new series of publications, LIFE Icons. With this and all succeeding books in the collection, we hope you glimpse the cover and feel that you've known that person for a good long time. Then we hope that, in the pages to follow, you come to know this iconic subject in a fresh, very personal way. That's our goal. We hope you'll feel we've succeeded.

# THE MAN

## with

*No Shirt*

Early on, as here in 1956, Hollywood saw beefcake. Clint had his eyes on something different from the get-go.

"I like to see somebody come out of the shadows and fool everybody with how good he is." The speaker in this instance is that fine actor Hal Holbrook, who costarred with Clint Eastwood in *Magnum Force*, the second of the five Dirty Harry movies Clint made between 1971 and 1988.

It's an important point, I think, and something of a forgotten one these days, when Clint is widely, and correctly, regarded as one of America's most important—and, for that matter, seemingly immortal—director-stars. But when you look at his nearly 60 years before the camera; consider all the Oscars and other major prizes he, his pictures and many of the actors who have worked on them have won; think about how beloved (and respected) so many of his films are; consider how well-liked and respected Clint himself is not only by the people who work with him but by the public at large, you realize that Holbrook raises a significant point, and one that can only be fully appreciated when you consider Clint's career from back to front, rather than the other way around. It's hard to believe, now, that Clint Eastwood came out of the shadows, but he did.

He was never a feckless young man. *Dutiful* is the word that comes more easily to mind. Clinton Eastwood Jr. was born in 1930 into a family that was occasionally hard pressed by the Depression. The Eastwoods led a wandering life as his father sought work and stability, a stability he would not achieve until wartime restored the family to relative prosperity. Clint amiably attended a technical high school in Oakland, entered the army (where he passed the time mostly as a swimming instructor), wandered about doing odd jobs for a while, then entered Los Angeles City College for a couple of convictionless semesters. If there was a center to his life in those years it was probably jazz. He played increasingly expert piano, but appears not to have thought of making a professional career in music.

He did marry, though, to Maggie Johnson, and, as important, he found a job that he rather liked.

Or thought he might come to like. It was in a talent program at Universal, which hired a number of young actors and actresses, offered them some training, occasionally a small role in one of their productions and a starting salary of $75 a week. The hope, of course, was that one or two of them might be noticed by the public and the studio would have a star (or demi-star) on the cheap. A cinematographer named Irving Glassberg, who had become friendly with the Eastwoods, set the deal up for Clint and as well introduced him to Arthur Lubin, a kindly and mildly competent director who had been on staff at

COURTESY KELLI ULDALL/CARMEL MAGAZINE

**GROWING UP** in the Bay Area, Clint inherited traits from both his parents that would allow him to make big, improbable leaps in the future. His father was a stockbroker brought down by the Depression who went to work in and around Oakland as a gas pumper/salesman/pipe fitter/you name it. From his dad, young Clint got his work ethic. His mother was the artistic one.

Universal for years. Lubin eventually made his largest fame and fortune as producer-director of the *Mister Ed* television series. Clint would talk to a lot of horses during his career, but only when guesting years later on Lubin's series did the horse talk back.

Clint fit comfortably into the program, though he was dubious about rising very far within it. He was, rather obviously, a good-looking young man, but also a rather shy one. He did not put himself forward in any obvious way and, anyway, he did not think he was of a type that was, at the time, finding favor with audiences. Tony Curtis, among others, was the beau ideal of the moment. No one then—not even Eastwood himself—was predicting stardom, let alone superstardom, for Clint. But he liked the camaraderie of the program. And he liked the opportunities it offered to learn something about the business he was increasingly interested in entering.

One of Clint's salient qualities is curiosity. When he is interested in something, he wants to know all about it. He began to visit sets at the studio, paying particular attention to the actors, but also noticing how the directors worked. It may be—he's not certain—that it was at this time the thought of someday directing occurred to him. Certainly he observed that all the power on a set flowed through that individual, that the actors, even when they were stars, were at his beck and call.

He had first begun auditing some acting classes in college and later began studying under a disciple of Michael Chekhov, nephew of the playwright Anton Chekhov and one of the leading students of the revolutionary and influential Russian acting teacher Constantin Stanislavski. The supposedly untutored cowboy actor of the 1950s and '60s was in fact a devoted student of his craft for several years, and I can attest: He remains today a voluble commentator on theories of acting.

So he paid attention and, meantime, he landed small roles in roughly a half dozen forgettable Universal films. He got a rather larger part courtesy of Lubin in *Francis in the Navy* (which—was this a precursor to *Mister Ed*?—starred a talking mule),

**RUTH EASTWOOD,** Clint's mother, who lived nearby in Carmel, California, until her death in 2006 at age 97, loved jazz and encouraged her boy as he learned to play piano and flugelhorn. Teenage Clint fancied himself a black kid trapped in a white kid's body, and this conceit was solidified when he saw Charlie Parker play in Oakland in 1946. Eastwood has been a backroom jazzman ever since. Here: At the keyboards in his Hollywood Hills home in 1965.

and he collected some rather agreeable endorsements from his teacher: "Cooperative, prompt, courteous and reliable," one of them read, continuing that "he gives promise of being one of the most conscientious boys we have ever had."

Clint wasn't so sure about his future at Universal, though he was also thinking that there was something right about his wanting to pursue acting as a career. He was correct on both counts. In September 1955, a one-sentence memo circulated at Universal. It read: "Please be advised that we will not exercise our option on Clint Eastwood."

On October 25, he worked his last day in the talent program (though not, as it would happen, his last day at Universal). Clint was not entirely surprised at the turn of events. Or particularly dismayed.

Maggie had a job that more or less supported them both, and, at least initially Clint had some prospects. Lubin had moved on to RKO, where in 1956 he was making *The First Traveling Saleslady*, starring Ginger Rogers. It was a rather mirthless comedy. But Clint had a decent part, got an "Introducing Clint Eastwood" credit and earned $750 for the job. He followed that with a much smaller role in *Escapade in Japan*, also for Lubin, and did a number of jobs in forgettable TV shows. He also dug an unconscionable number of swimming pools to help make ends meet,

This was, it can be said in retrospect, the low point in his acting career. Roles were rare and not very promising. Yet from such a low, things can only go up. The turning point, such as it was, was the enthusiasm William A. Wellman showed for him. The veteran and expert director was about to make his last picture, *Lafayette Escadrille*, a semiautobiography recounting the director's years as a member of the Lafayette Flying Corps. He favored Clint for the lead. Clint loved the rough-hewn director, and this was the first time he was up for the lead in an A picture. But the studio was more than skeptical and, in the end, the part was given to boyish Tab Hunter. Wellman felt terrible about getting Clint's hopes up and cast him as a member of the ensemble of flyers supporting Hunter. He was okay in the role, but somewhat lost in the shuffle of supporting players, and the film itself turned out to be, if I can put it kindly, routine fare.

Later in 1958, Clint got what amounted to the heroic lead in a quickie western, *Ambush at Cimarron Pass*. This turned out to be not entirely okay, not at all. The film was about a group of unhorsed wayfarers in Indian Country—imagine a western totally devoid of horses—and starred an entirely charmless actor, Scott Brady. It precipitated something of a crisis in the Eastwood household. Eventually, it was to be

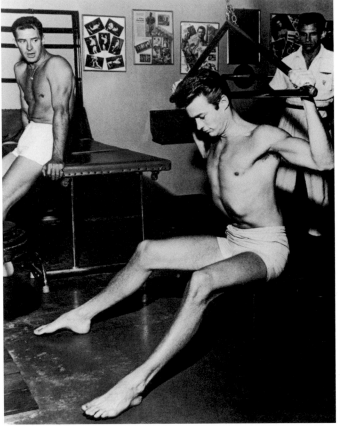

LOU VALENTINO COLLECTION

**CLINT'S MOTHER** was hale and hearty to a good old age, and Clint, a lifelong fitness buff, has remained so himself. Back in the day, the studio liked the shirtless shots of him lifting, but these didn't need to be staged—he has lifted his whole life, though it was less than necessary during his hard-labor years as a lumberjack and then the years in the Army. A fine swimmer, during the Korean War he served stateside as a swimming instructor—and when a plane he was on crashed, he swam three miles to safety.

released, slated as the bottom half of a double bill. Clint and Maggie betook themselves to the theater on opening day, with Clint slumping down lower and lower in his seat. "It probably looked like Maggie was sitting alone," he told me. She tried to be supportive, but Clint was inconsolable as he watched "this pile of crap run by." He is of the opinion that it was the worst movie ever made. It was not, of course; it was just another bad movie, of which there are, obviously, very many. Nevertheless, he recalled thinking, "This is just dog----." He wondered if perhaps it was time to give up the acting dream. "I started thinking, I'm going back to school. I'm going to learn something. I'm going to get some other kind of a job. I'm going to jump out of this."

But he didn't.

And his luck was about to definitively turn.

A friend of his, Sonia Chernus, was working at CBS as a reader, and wanted to introduce him to a woman who might do his career some good. So Clint dropped in there early in the summer of 1958, had the meeting (to no particular good effect) and was strolling down the hall when a man named Robert Sparks happened to pop out of an office. He asked Clint if he was an actor. Clint said yes and was invited into an office where he began to exaggerate his credits. Soon enough, Charles Marquis Warren, head writer and producer of a new western series to be called *Rawhide* was asked to join them, and they started talking about this western that Warren was working up. For once, Clint seemed to be right for a part others had in mind: the young and innocent second in command on a show that every season would feature a cattle drive from Texas to a railhead in Missouri. His character, Rowdy Yates, Clint later described as the "idiot of the plains." But it was a running part, and westerns, at that time, were TV's hottest genre, filling something like a quarter of prime-time network schedules. There was no pressing need for another one, but, on the other hand, no reason not to do one, either.

Events moved rapidly. Clint did an interview and a reading, and that was it. He was hired (at $700 an episode), a pilot was made, and starting in January of '59, a full complement of shows (13 in all) was shot and slipped into the CBS schedule. Here, at last, was steady work.

*Rawhide* conformed to most expected norms. For instance, it had, as many westerns did, a raucous theme song and a snarling trail boss (played by Eric Fleming, who grew disaffected with the program as the years wore on). But it also had, in Clint Eastwood, an advantage that many of its competitors did not. He was young, handsome and very appealing to

young women. This was not missed by the network nor by Clint, and if the actor kept his shirt on while filming, as a cowboy must, it often seemed to go missing during photo shoots. Clint's shyness, too, was appealing, and *Rawhide*'s audience had a surprising demographic for a western, a lot of females in the mix.

The show would run on and on—seven years— never a huge hit, but relatively inexpensive to produce and pulling its modest weight in the ratings. On a weekly basis, Clint Eastwood grew a little more famous. He was tall in the saddle, riding toward a future no one would have—or could have—predicted.

CBS PHOTO ARCHIVE/GETTY

**CLINT LANDED** *Rawhide,* which debuted in January 1959, and before long the show was in the ratings top 20 (above, Clint in 1961, when *Rawhide* was at the peak of its success, finishing at number six for the 1960–61 season). Clint often worked six-day weeks as an actor on the show, 12 or more hours some days, and even directed some trailers for *Rawhide.* The producers refused to let him direct a full episode though.

**HERE IN 1955,** Clint (center in the picture at right; right at top; third from left in the center photo; and center rear, above) and his Universal Studios classmates are learning their chops. The vicissitudes of Tinseltown can be appreciated by taking a quick look at the careers of some of the others in these pictures. In the photo above, John Agar—listening at far left as Tony Curtis, in the white T-shirt, imparts his sage wisdom— did westerns (*Fort Apache* and *She Wore a Yellow Ribbon* with John Wayne), then B fare like *The Mole People* and *Tarantula*. (He was also Shirley Temple's first husband). Gia Scala, with Clint at top and at right, made *The Guns of Navarone* with Gregory Peck in 1961 but died young after battling drugs and alcohol. John Saxon, far right in the middle photo, is still working after more than 200 projects over the years, and is remembered as a cop in *A Nightmare on Elm Street*.

LARRY BARBIER/GLOBE/Z JMA (3)

**THE YEAR IS 1961** and Clint is a TV star. He had met Maggie Johnson on a blind date in the early summer of 1953, and they were wed before year's end; their marriage would last more than a quarter century, but was checkered with episodes emblematic of the actor's complicated love life. His first child, Kimber, was born in 1964 to the actress Roxanne Tunis. After he and Johnson had reconciled, she gave birth to Kyle in 1968 and Alison in 1972. The couple finally divorced in 1984. By today, Clint has seven children by five women, two of whom he was married to. "The fact that I am only the second woman he has married really touches me," said Dina Ruiz after their 1996 wedding. Said Maggie at one point, "He had this thing about being a loner, like I didn't exist. He's a very complex person."

**MORE CLINT AND MAGGIE** at home, dancing next to a turntable and a rack full of records in the living room, then Clint, with his discerning taste, choosing the next cut. Note the Lacoste polo shirt and penny loafers, not worn by accident. Many years later, in 1997, when Clint, famous as an avocational golfer, started a line of golf wear, his was the antithesis of Tiger Woods's sleek Nike gear: It was classical, even retro, and extremely clean; it was what you saw Arnold Palmer wearing in those terrific black-and-white photos from the early 1960s—or Clint wearing for a home shoot.

# THE MAN
## with
## NO NAME

By the time Clint made
*The Good, The Bad and the Ugly*
in 1966, his cheroot and
scowl were firmly in place, as was
his limitless future.

**C**lint got tired of *Rawhide* after a time, but the money was good—better as the years wore on and he was presumptively a star—and so he stuck with it. The series would eventually have to end, of course, but when it did Clint would still be young, with options in front of him. Clint was sanguine about it all, and smart. He deferred a substantial part of his TV salary, so that he would not have to take the first job that came along when *Rawhide* was cancelled. The actor was always shrewder, more prudent, than Rowdy Yates looked. Image influences much in Hollywood, and it took folks a while to realize they shouldn't underestimate Clint Eastwood.

As it happened, Clint's fiscal self-discipline was unnecessary. His agents at William Morris had received an offer for a picture then called *The Magnificent Stranger:* A western. Shot in Spain. With an Italian director. Who did not speak English. Clint was not interested. But the Rome office of William Morris had promised he would look at it. So over it came—a strange-looking script, on onionskin paper, a fourth or fifth carbon copy with notes looking more like the outline of a novel than a conventional screenplay. Clint glanced at it and immediately recognized it as a knockoff of Akira Kurosawa's *Yojimbo,* a film he had admired and had always thought was a good candidate for remaking as a western, which it basically was anyway in all but setting.

**CLINT IS ON THE SET** of *A Fistful of Dollars* with director Sergio Leone and actress Margarita Lozano. There was not even a fine line between high art and base commerce in postwar European cinema; Lozano, for instance, worked not only with Leone but also Buñuel and Pasolini—and it was all good. It would take a while for Leone's masterworks, slandered as "spaghetti westerns" by U.S. arbiters, to be given their due, but Clint knew they were worthy—if different—from the start.

© MPTV IMAGES

Although it was about a samurai, Kurosawa had been greatly influenced by American westerns and films noir, so this was everything coming around.

The document was, by the time it reached Clint's hands, well traveled. A number of action stars had passed on it, mostly because the producers could not come up with the $25,000 fee they wanted. Clint had no hesitation. There was a hiatus from *Rawhide* coming up and he was weary of the show's blandness in any case. He had never been abroad, and he thought it might be kind of fun to go to Europe and see how they did things over there. Mostly, though, he liked the idea that his character was the direct opposite of Rowdy Yates—a tough, grizzled, almost terminally laconic figure. "The Man With No Name," as he came to be known, was in every respect unlike the character Clint had been playing on television. (The character actually had a name in all three of the pictures made by the virtually unknown Sergio Leone; the "no name" angle was the invention of a nameless marketing man.) There seemed no downside. Money was no object to Clint. He literally had nothing better to do. The classic American western was, he told me later, in "a dead space," soft and nostalgic and largely in the hands of aging masters like John Ford. It could use some new blood, some new vigor, some new action.

So, then: If, on the face of it, he had nothing in particular to gain from this enterprise, well, he didn't have anything at all to lose from it, either.

Off he went, carrying the guns and other gear he used on *Rawhide;* several boxes of foul cigars ("they put you in the right mood, cantankerous"), which became his character's trademark; and a determination to shake things up.

It is hard to explain how or why Clint was even in contention for this role. He had done nothing remotely resembling the character that he was being considered for on-screen. One gets the feeling that the Italians had about run out of logical choices for the part and were now willing to look into the illogical ones. About all Clint had going for him was that he was a television star, which might help at the North America box office, should the film happen to have one.

It is only in retrospect that the choice of Eastwood appears to have been almost heaven-sent. For the truth is that The Man With No Name is closer to Clint's true nature than Rowdy Yates ever was—an ironist, even at times a humorist, and a man now in his mid-thirties who could look the part. He was tall, lean and, with the beard he wore for the part, more than capable of a grizzled air. A little bit of a cynic, but also a little bit of a secret idealist. Put a poncho on him and he was perfectly cast.

**A MEASURE** of how far Clint had come, and how quickly, is that by 1968 he was not only making his westerns in Hollywood, but coproducing them with his newly formed company, Malpaso (which means "bad step" in Spanish, and is also the name of a creek on his property in Monterey County, California). The first of these movies was *Hang 'Em High* (above, a publicity still), a fine bit of shoot-'em-up melodrama. Clint chose Ted Post, who had helmed more than two dozen *Rawhide* episodes, to direct. A good chunk of the cast, including Ed Begley, Bruce Dern and Pat Hingle, were *Rawhide* veterans as well.

Clint took a liking to Leone, who turned out to be a voluble, volatile character, a short, chubby man—physically Clint's direct opposite—who had learned his craft as an assistant on many an Italian epic. Clint and the director did not share a language, but Leone loved acting out Clint's role, and the actor loved the director's enthusiasm and his willingness to break with the hoary conventions of the western, some of which Leone wasn't even aware of (Clint refusing to enlighten him). All in all, they had a good time in Almería, Spain, in conditions that didn't feature so much as a rest room. "We just went out behind the rocks," Clint says. It's a good thing, perhaps, that the cast was largely male; The Man with No Name trilogy would be a testosterone-fueled series.

Clint returned to the United States pleased enough with the work they—and he   had done. There ensued a lengthy silence, but then word began drifting out of Europe. The picture—now entitled *A Fistful of Dollars* and greatly enhanced by Ennio Morricone's brilliant score, which is seen today as having boosted the musical possibilities of all movies—had opened in Italy and was turning into a huge hit there. Soon enough a print was sent to Clint, and he screened it for a group of his friends, who were pleased by it. Now producers came calling, seeking Clint's participation in a sequel, which seemed a good idea to him. Eventually two of them were made—*For a Few Dollars More* and *The Good, the Bad and the Ugly*—and they were released by United Artists in 1967 and then '68. All three films met with thunderous critical disapproval.

Renata Adler, beginning her short stint as a *New York Times* critic with some words about *The Good, the Bad and the Ugly*, voiced an entirely typical opinion. "[T]he most expensive, pious and repellent movie in the history of its peculiar genre," she wrote. This sentiment was echoed almost everywhere across the country. Nearly half a century after the fact of the trilogy, it is hard for me to see what all the outrage was about. The original picture and the next two are certainly tough and fairly brutal, but not unbearably so. Their major sin was to question the comfortable pieties—the rote morality—that had ruled the western genre for decades. It turned out, if I can analyze it from the current vantage, that the reviewers were more committed to the status quo than they were willing to admit. Or: had to admit, given that no one, until this point, had occasion or reason to question the genre's sleepy conventions.

The audience had no such compunctions. *A Fistful of Dollars* and its sequels stirred the people in the seats. Now that they were exposed to this alternative take on the western, they decided that they liked the transgressiveness of Leone's work. It had plenty of rough action, and rough wit, too, and they enjoyed all of it. Besides, in the end the films came down on the side of conventional morality.

Put simply, an American genre had been kick-started by a bunch of folks working in 110-degree heat and having a great time of it over in Europe (the desert scenes in *For a Few Dollars More* and *The Good, the Bad and the Ugly* were shot across the street from Leone's ranch). These people sent back to America's movie houses The Man with No Name and his quiet crusades, and the public responded explosively. They didn't give a hoot what the critics thought. They simply enjoyed the show. As much as anything, they enjoyed the blunt ironies of the *Dollars* trilogy. They could take the movies seriously—but not too seriously.

As for Clint, he delighted in the rumpus. He had gone to Europe as a minor television star. He had been making a decent living playing a sweet-spirited naïf—what had become for him a rather boring role. He now came back with his screen persona utterly transformed. He was transitioning from Rowdy Yates to Clint Eastwood. Oh, those silences! That squint!

I would argue that in the entire history of the medium no one had ever made a more radical transformation of his screen image than this one. And it had been a great move. Clint was suddenly more or less a movie star. Not yet a great one, but surely a comer: a man on his way. Suddenly, the American studios were taking an interest in him. They didn't know quite what he had. But he had something. That much they could see.

CAMERA PRESS/SORCI/REDUX

© MPTV IMAGES

**IN THE MID-1960S,** Clint was an even bigger star in Europe than he was in America, and he enjoyed his time abroad. Above he is on the Via Veneto in Rome in 1965 during the filming of *For a Few Dollars More,* and at right he tours London during the 1968 shooting of *Where Eagles Dare.* It was nothing new by this point that Clint, while known to be a married man (but one with a reputation), drew the attention, and affections, of female fans. In fact, he was a father by now—though the paternity of this first child was not made public until the late 1980s—from his affair with Roxanne Tunis.

**WHETHER HE** simply enjoyed stretching in his roles, or whether he took pride in doing so, is a question Clint will modestly dismiss. But the man who later would assay the romantic lead in *The Bridges of Madison County* and direct more than a couple of comedies took an early leap in 1969 when he made the terrific Lerner and Loewe musical *Paint Your Wagon* alongside fellow gruffneck Lee Marvin. In these intimate photographs taken during down time on the Oregon shoot, Clint chills with a fly rod and a guitar, perhaps developing a strategy for his vocalization on the ballad "I Still See Elisa." He couldn't sing, not a lick, but he sold his songs with gusto and grit. He would contribute much music to future films, including his own compositions, and would be nominated for a Best Score Grammy for 2004's *Million Dollar Baby.* But never again would he warble on film.

**HERE,** Clint gets some hands-on filmmaking experience during the shooting of the 1968 movie *Coogan's Bluff,* directed by Don Siegel. This was the first of their five collaborations over the next several years. Clint had returned to Universal Studios because of an acting fee—$1 million—that was twice his previous high, and there he met the contract director Siegel. The two hit it off immediately, and would become close friends. Working on *Bluff,* Eastwood also met jazz-steeped composer Lalo Schifrin, who would, like Siegel, distinguish several Eastwood vehicles throughout the 1970s. *Coogan's Bluff* dealt with an Arizona lawman chasing a psychopathic criminal to (and through) New York City, and was somewhat controversial for its violence. Siegel and Eastwood, who shortly enough would cocreate *Dirty Harry,* hadn't heard anything yet.

EVERETT

NO BETS
ON TABLE

**ON TWO MORE** Don Siegel–directed films, Clint acted, continued his well-funded apprenticeship, and clearly itched to be in charge one day, one day soon. Above, the two men are on the set of 1970's *Two Mules for Sister Sara,* a western that costarred Shirley MacLaine. Clint could have sleepwalked through his role: a mysterious cigar-chomping stranger in a serape who, we know from the outset, will win the day. Opposite: On the set of *The Beguiled.* Clint later blamed that movie's poor box office performance in part on his conflicted, "emasculated" character, and told author Patrick McGilligan while discussing *The Beguiled* (which Richard Schickel will address further on the pages following), "Dustin Hoffman and Al Pacino play losers very well. But my audience likes to be in there vicariously with a winner. That isn't always popular with the critics. My characters have sensitivity and vulnerabilities, but they're still winners. I don't pretend to understand losers. When I read a script about a loser I think of people in life who are losers and they seem to want it that way. It's a compulsive philosophy with them. Winners tell themselves, I'm as bright as the next person. I can do it. Nothing can stop me." Nothing would stop Clint Eastwood, that was for sure.

# THE MAN

## with a

# BIG GUN

## ... and an Orangutan

He asked the bad guys
to make his day, even as he
made ours. God help us all,
we loved Dirty Harry.

**B**y the time *The Good, The Bad and the Ugly* was finished in 1966, Clint was 36 years old, rather late in the day to emerge as a full-fledged movie star. I think he knew that he had to catch up. As important—maybe more so—he was a star only to the public. Among the finer sensibilities keeping track of cinema's progress he was, facts being faced, a widely deplored figure. The wit and style of the Leone films—the revolutionary effect they had on their genre—had simply not been acknowledged by the arbiters of the art form. All anyone in the intelligensia could see, or talk about, was their violence.

I don't know whether it was a conscious strategy or not, but what Clint did in the next three years, from 1968 to 1971, was to busy himself. He made nine films in those years. They were in virtually all genres (even including a musical), which was certainly part of the plan, whatever the grand plan was. Clint didn't want to be fully associated with the action genre.

The results were excellent. By the end of this period, he had begun his collaboration with his most beloved of directorial mentors, Don Siegel; achieved legitimate stardom (though not yet the endorsement of the critical establishment); made his first film as a director; and capped things off with a picture that converted his stardom to superstardom, *Dirty Harry*. Since he wasn't winning over the tastemakers, he had taken his case straight to the people. Many years later, he asked his longtime friend and publicist, Joe Hyams, "How many pictures did Clark Gable make?" That, of course, was the point: You want to make yourself inevitable as a movie star, someone whose name occurs to everyone when the subject comes up. It doesn't make as much difference if the pictures are good rather than bad or indifferent (well, not too many in the latter categories) as long as you work steadily in pictures, associating your name with an above-the-title stardom that, eventually, is unquestioned: the actor as an accepted part of the movie cosmos.

Of the nine films Clint made in these years, five were relatively straightforward action pieces—none of which are discreditable—and most were modestly profitable, some greatly so. Three of them were, in their different ways, extraordinary. Set aside, for the moment, *Dirty Harry* and concentrate on *The Beguiled* and *Play Misty for Me*, a flop and a modest success, both of which did a daring thing: They questioned the premises of the star's masculinity—in fact, of masculinity as it had been traditionally portrayed in the movies since time immemorial.

Take *The Beguiled*, directed with assurance and ease by Siegel. In it Clint plays a union soldier trapped and wounded behind Confederate lines in the Civil War, then rescued and tended to by the teachers and students of a ladies seminary. He can't believe his good luck. The women, led by a headmistress played very well by Geraldine Page, are, to put it decorously, sexually restless, and, in his arrogant masculine way, Clint's character aims to have his way with as many of them as possible. This looks to him like heaven in the midst of wartime hell. But these women are deadlier than the male. First, his allegedly gangrenous leg is amputated. Finally, he is killed by poison. The poor sap never knew what hit him. Sure: It's Southern Gothic. But the undermining of Clint Eastwood's cocksurety is wonderful to behold. To offer a critique of simple-minded maleness within the confines of a genre picture remains even now a startling thing, but Clint was onboard with it. In the movie, Clint never acknowledges what is happening to him until it is too late, and then there is room only for panic; it was as if this film's Clint was finally looking at the earlier Clint of the audience's expectation. The film was a rare commercial failure for him. The audience was not ready for this kind of dubiety from an action hero.

**AS LONG AS** he was able, Clint preferred not to use a stunt man and to perform his own feats of derring-do. When he was making the first of the five Dirty Harry films, he was still not so much of a priceless commodity that he would be held back by producers or directors—certainly not by his pal Siegel. And so Harry Callahan leaps from a railroad trestle to the top of a bus as the camera rolls.

*Play Misty for Me*, his next picture and his directorial debut, was written by a friend, Jo Heims, and Clint had it under option for a while. It eventually passed to Universal, which casually permitted him to direct it—for the minimum directing salary. That was all right with Clint; he said, in fact, that he ought to pay them for the chance to prove himself. He had been looking through lenses on movie sets since working with Leone, and Siegel not only encouraged him in his aspirations, but coached him when he

JOHN BRYSON/SYGMA/CORBIS

**IN THE 1970S,** the newly confirmed superstar changed hats on a picture-by-picture basis: actor, director, actor-director; starring in thrillers, westerns (including the classic *The Outlaw Josey Wales*), three Harrys, comedies, films without category (*The Beguiled*). He was working all the time, heading for divorce at last from Maggie, beginning his fraught relationship with Sondra Locke, trying to be there for his kids. If he never seemed at loose ends—Clint simply couldn't, wouldn't—then his life must have been every which way but loose.

had the time. Now, apprenticed, Clint took the helm.

In *Misty* he plays Dave Garver, a small-town jazz disc jockey ambitious for bigger things, but meantime exploiting what the area has to offer in the way of female companionship. To him Evelyn Draper (played by Jessica Walter with wonderfully controlled lunacy) is just another casual conquest. Dave does not recognize that Evelyn does not do casual. She does do attempted murder, though, after Dave tries to keep her in her place. It is a minor film, perhaps, but a really scary one—just the right scale and kind for a directorial debut.

To briefly return to the subject of Clint's boldness in playing against type. Dave is a smug man. He's got his little world under his command. It is fine to see cool Clint Eastwood lose that treasured, centered life. How many stars would risk, especially at such a relatively early stage in their careers, that loss of command—command being the action hero's stock in trade? It is also fine to see the director's assured handling of this film, as he begins a career of directing himself. I think that, Woody Allen aside, no one in the history of feature films has more often done that trick. Clint's capacity and willingness to objectify himself without dither or self-doubt—so often, and usually to such good effect—remains unparalleled.

The only misstep that arose in the actor-director duality during this first foray was comical. The day before the shoot began, Clint worked hard to assure there were no foreseeable problems, and he went to bed pleased with his efforts. He had just turned out the light, when he found himself bolting upright. He had forgotten that he had to act in some of the next day's scenes. He snapped on the light and began memorizing his lines, perhaps thinking he was in trouble with his director.

The picture, which was shot on a shoestring in Carmel, California, where Clint had already established his principal residence, did well. His friend and colleague Steven Spielberg, says he immediately recognized that Clint was a directorial force, a man capable of tight, taut screen storytelling. Don Siegel surely felt the same when he saw *Misty*.

**AFTER DIRTY HARRY,** Clint was unquestionably an A-lister, and so it was natural for him and Paul Newman to hang casually during a chance meeting outside a motel in Tucson in 1972. How big was Clint in this period? When Sean Connery announced he wouldn't play James Bond again, the coveted role was offered to Clint. He turned it down, saying it didn't feel right, and that year he made the western *Joe Kidd* instead. In a sign that the intense glare was perhaps getting to him, he reportedly suffered an anxiety attack during shooting.

Incidentally, he had come up to play a small role in the film as a bartender, his presence for Clint more talismanic than vital.

This brings us to *Dirty Harry,* which Clint did not direct; Siegel did—and very well, too. This is the film that was, after *A Fistful of Dollars,* a second huge game-changer for Clint. As with *Fistful,* it's lucky that it came his way. The script (more properly many scripts) had been floating around for awhile. Paul Newman had once been interested, but finally found it politically incorrect. Frank Sinatra was interested for a much longer time, but, it was reported, passed because of an injury to his hand. The latest screenplay treatments were now at Warner Bros., where Clint's

friend and lawyer, Frank Wells, was an executive. He knew of Clint's interest, and sent over the script. Actually, in Clint's words, "a whole mess of scripts," only one of which interested him—the original, written by Harry Julian Fink and his wife, Rita. Eventually polished by Dean Riesner (and other hands as well), this became the shooting script Siegel used.

Clint knew from the outset that the movie was bound to be "controversial," but didn't much care about that. On the most basic level he saw *Dirty Harry* as a first-class cop drama, with the not unusual aspect of having its protagonist at odds with his superiors' bureaucratic dithering over the rights of criminals—at the expense, of course, of the rights of their victims. In this case, too much trouble was being taken over *Miranda* rights, a matter much in the news in 1971 when the picture was released.

I don't think the average moviegoer paid much attention to that issue; they were preoccupied with the duel between Harry Callahan and "Scorpio," a first-rate villain personified by the snarling psychopathy of Andy Robinson's brilliant performance. Here was an opponent who would test the competence of our movie hero (or antihero) in ways few bad guys ever do. Harry and Scorpio's well-paced duel, spread across the movie in well-placed increments, makes you forget, much of the time, the troublesome aspects of Harry's relationship to Scorpio's *Miranda* rights. We always understand that this particular villian is a very special case. Clint/Harry certainly understands that. And he really doesn't give a rat's ass about reading this punk his rights.

Some critics, however, did. *The New Yorker*'s Pauline Kael, exhibiting for the first time what would be a lifelong enmity toward all of Clint's work, called the movie "fascist medievalism" and personalized the sociological attack by misidentifying Clint as some sort of John Wayne clone. (In real life, he is not, of course; he is, rather, a sort of fiscal conservative who is as liberal as anyone might wish on matters involving civil liberties. As a matter of fact, Harry Callahan is no more than a half-step advanced on the long movie tradition of pissed-off cops at odds

KEN REGAN/CAMERA 5

EVERETT

**OPPOSITE:** Dad swings Kyle on the set of *Dirty Harry* in 1971 and, then, Alison in 1983. No role has he taken more seriously than that of father, even as he admits his route to such a large brood—the seven-children-with-five-different-women thing—has been unorthodox. He's sly and coy and humorous about this, as he is about most things. "I've never had so much fun with the father thing, never enjoyed doing the father thing more"—pause—"and I've done it a few times."

**CLINT AND KYLE** play in 1977; and he and Alison cuddle in 1984 on the set of the harrowing thriller *Tightrope*, in which they play father and daughter. If he has allowed his older children to choose show business should they so desire—and he has—he has nonetheless tried to shield them when he can. He has made an earnest effort to forge some kind of nuclear family out of one that is far-flung in so many ways.

DOUGLAS JONES/GLOBE/ZUMA (3).

**"I DON'T THINK** I've had anybody look at me like that before. It's a real Clint Eastwood look. It's intimidating. You let me know, 'Approach with caution.'" So said Steve Kroft on *60 Minutes* in 1997 after asking his guest, Clint Eastwood, about his family. Clint explained his wariness, and his expression: "Well, 'cause I—you—they're—there are other people that are involved there, and they're vulnerable people. I can protect myself, but they can't." On these pages: The family on the set of *High Plains Drifter* in 1972.

KEN REGAN/CAMERA 5 (2)

**CLINT, KYLE AND ALISON** in the mid-1980s. Kyle, Maggie's son, born in 1968, is today an accomplished jazz musician, and credits both his parents for his love of music, recalling that they dug (as they then said) Miles Davis, Dave Brubeck, Thelonious Monk and the Stan Kenton Big Band, and that the family used to attend the Monterey Jazz Festival, where, as Clint's kid, he could meet the stars backstage. Alison, Maggie's daughter, born in 1972, is still an actress as well as a director, fashion model and clothing designer.

**IN THE 1975 MOVIE** *The Eiger Sanction,* directed by and starring Eastwood, Clint took his penchant for doing his own stunts to extremes. He trained in mountain climbing in Yosemite before filming began in Switzerland, but his insistence on tackling the rock face of the Eiger was disapproved by members of the production. An experienced climber hired as a body double was in fact killed during a fall, and a cameraman was injured in another fall. Eastwood later explained to film critic Roger Ebert why he was so insistent that he dangle from the cliff: "I wanted to use a telephoto lens and zoom in slowly all the way to my face—so you could see it was really me. I put on a little disguise and slipped into a sneak preview of the film to see how people liked it. When I was hanging up there in the air, the woman in front of me said to her friend, 'Gee, I wonder how they did that?' and her friend said, 'Special effects.'"

FRANK EDWARDS/FOTOS INTERNATIONAL/GETTY

EVA SERENY/CAMERA PRESS/REDUX

© 1978 GARY LEWIS/MPTV IMAGES

**DOING HIS OWN STUNTS** on the 13,025-foot-high Eiger in the Swiss Alps may be extreme, but physical activity has always been a part of Clint's life, from swimming through tennis and skiing to golf, which remains important to him. This page, clockwise from top left: Lucille Ball and her husband, Gary Morton, socialize with Clint at a tennis tournament in Carlsbad, California, circa 1970; Clint practices in 1974; Clint and James Brolin in the '70s. Opposite: Staring down an approach shot circa 1975.

© GARY LEWIS/MPTV IMAGES

**GETTING HIMSELF**
out of trouble at the AT&T
celebrity pro-am golf tournament.
"I play golf maybe three times
a week," Clint said in 1999 as he
approached his 70th birthday. "It's
good to have recreations. I don't
overanalyze them." At the time he
was still jogging, lifting. He was
in his third decade of practicing
transcendental meditation. He
has never smoked, not even as No
Name did he inhale, and he gorges
on vitamins. There are, as we have
already seen, a lot of surprises
with Clint Eastwood, but he won't
help you get all metaphysical
about them. "I don't necessarily
see similarities in the things
I choose to do. Maybe rhythm.
Golf, music—they have rhythm in
common." Clint wouldn't admit
to being much of a golfer, but he
was and is a good one, playing
to a handicap of about a dozen as
he turned 70, with an athlete's
smooth swing. "I like everything
about the game," he said that
day, and paused to survey the
beautiful, brand-new golf course
he was playing, high above the
Pacific—a course he had just
finished building as a club for
himself and his best friends.
"I love playing around here."

**CLINT'S EASE** on a set is only greater when he is a hired hand—not directing—as here, during the filming of *Joe Kidd.* This production was in the charge of John Sturges, with whom Clint had longed to work, and featured a screenplay by Elmore Leonard. Clint's costar was the estimable Robert Duvall, and billed third was one of his old pals from the Universal Studios acting class, John Saxon. All these good vibes, but the film itself wasn't as good as it could have been.

# THE MAN

## with the

# CAMERA

Other directors may wear fancy hats and kerchiefs to the set. When Clint is dressed a bit unconventionally as he peers through the lens, it's because he has another job to do—out front.

Clint had been with Warner Bros. since 1976, and he had built a unique partnership in working with the studio. Martin Scorsese correctly says that Clint's way hearkens back to older studio days, when directors tended to be under multipicture contracts and worked closely with their studio's executives, building careers for the long term. Clint's arrangement, based on a handshake, endures to this day—36 years and counting. It is unprecedented in the history of Hollywood.

Clint's method of work, too, is largely without precedent. He has only once "developed" a film. He buys finished scripts on the open market, with friends and colleagues keeping a vigilant eye out for suitable projects. He may occasionally suggest changes in the documents he buys, but they are usually very few. As for shooting his films, his style is unique. He casts by looking at videos. On set, he moves fast—usually two or three takes at most—and quietly. He doesn't say, "Action" (usually it's something like "Whenever you're ready"), and he doesn't say, "Cut" (it's more likely "Okay"). He is available to his actors if they need to talk something over, but basically they are present in the first place because he knows they can do their jobs, and so he doesn't say much. The atmosphere on an Eastwood production is as serene as possible considering that a multimillion-dollar movie is being made on deadline. The food is always good on his sets, and he joins the chow line just like everyone else. He interacts with the crew as readily as with the stars. Mostly everyone is anticipating his moves, and everyone proceeds with great good humor. He does have a temper and, though he rarely shows it, it is terrible to behold. But it is always directed at mechanical elements that go wrong, not at individuals. Actors and crew simply swear by him—I've never met anyone who doesn't want to work for Clint a second or third or 20th time—and so do Warner Bros. execs. As a result of his process, Clint is invariably under budget, ahead of schedule and, once the tickets start selling, in the black. None of this behavior appears to have been learned: He has worked this way since his directorial debut. The conditions are those he would choose when he is acting, so they are based on good instinct as well as personal character.

Clint's relationship with Warner Bros. is so solid that by the mid-1980s he could suggest doing a picture the studio would be sure to want—an action piece of some sort—and then one that might satisfy his own yearnings to try something more aspirational. I think his purely popular pictures in this period were, on the whole, of a lower quality than they had been earlier—but then, he was somewhat distracted. He was serving his term as mayor of Carmel, a small-town job that drew national attention, and his relationship with Sondra Locke was not going well. They would break up, rather nastily, in 1989.

And yet there was the highly original western *Pale Rider* in 1985, and a passion project, *Bird*, a biopic of jazzman Charlie Parker, in 1988. The darkest of all of Clint's pictures, controversial in jazz circles, a movie with small hope of profitability (which was all right with the studio), *Bird*, with a fine performance by Forest Whitaker as Parker, showed what Eastwood

WARNER BROS./EVERETT

**NO ONE** expected *Bird* to earn a lot of money, but Clint wanted to make it, and by 1988 most anything he wanted to make, he could. He drew fine performances from Forest Whitaker (left) in the title role and Sam Wright, here on set with their director. None of Clint's films in his later years were vanity projects; he was trying to make good movies about interesting subjects, and few things inspired him as much as jazz and Charlie Parker's music, which had changed him when he first saw Parker play in Oakland way back in '46.

could do when he stretched. And there was also *Heartbreak Ridge*, in 1986: Clint playing Tom Highway, a marine non-com serving his last tour of duty and hoping to reconcile with his wife (an excellent Marsha Mason), a man trying his damnedest to find the rhythms of the new, softer masculinity, and basically failing miserably. Later Clint and his good friend Gene Hackman were talking about how he might have done some of his best work in the movie, and a fair number of critics agreed.

Sometimes it seemed incongruous. The same man who made *Heartbreak Ridge* would deliver, four years later, *White Hunter, Black Heart.* The character Clint plays, John Wilson, is based on the director John Huston, and the performance is rich in pompous macho posturing. What Clint hoped would be a serious contemplation of Hemingwayesque machismo left audiences puzzled and unhappy, and the picture was pretty much dumped by the studio, a rare occurance in Clint's career. And the same man who made *Bird* also made *Pink Cadillac* and *The Rookie,* both rather empty comedies. There are times, Clint admits, that buying scripts on the open market is not productive, and this was a period when that cupboard was pretty bare. He was now 60 years old and people around the business were wondering if, at last, his time was running out. A newspaper article referred to him as a "fading house star" at Warner Bros.

But he and a few close friends knew something his critics did not. He had been savoring for some years a script that would change, if not his life, then his career. This would be a third game-changer, to join *A Fistful of Dollars* and *Dirty Harry.*

Clint said that the film eventually to be called *Unforgiven* was, in screenplay form, "something I could sit on and bank and I kind of hung on to it like a nice little gold watch." Other times he thought of it as a treat, a "little plum I was savoring . . . something good on your plate and you're saying 'I'll eat this last.'" One thing was for certain: He was going to make a movie out of David Webb Peoples's script, which he had read as a sample of the writer's work back in 1983 and had waited for many years to produce.

KEN REGAN/CAMERA 5

**IN 1986** Mayor Clint smiles in the charming California town where he lives and now, after a fashion, rules. The actor-director certainly didn't need a third gig, but just as surely he had long been a man of opinions—an eclectic collection of opinions, ranging from right to left, with many close to the center—and so he raised his hand. One term would be enough, and then it was back to the day job(s).

He said he wanted to be older to play Will Munny, and, truth be told, he may have thought of the role as something that could turn his career around when and if it hit a downturn. For whatever reason, in the spring of 1991 the time seemed right to him. He called Peoples and said he was going into production in the fall. He fooled around with some changes a bit, then told the writer he was going to shoot it as written. Peoples was as relieved as he was pleased; like everyone in his trade, he was all too familiar with what happens when stars start "improving" scripts.

The studio encouraged Clint to employ top actors to support him (in the event, Gene Hackman, Morgan Freeman, Richard Harris). He and his cast and crew headed to a ranch a couple of hours from Calgary, in Canada, which became the rude western town called Big Whiskey. Presided over by a sadistic

sheriff (Hackman) who is psychopathically a law-and-order man, Big Whiskey is a place waiting for bad things to happen. Munny, once a feared gunslinger, is now—he thinks—a reformed man, helped along by a good woman. His intention is to earn a reward for killing two drunken cowboys who had cut a whore in the course of a night's carousing. Of course, things aren't going to unspool quite as planned.

There are many riches in this tale (including a fine use of period language), and an air of fatedness hangs over the whole enterprise, which is very darkly realized. Clint and the studio played the prerelease very low key—just another western and all that. Peoples saw an early screening of the final print, thought it wonderful and then wondered if he had written a picture only its makers could love. It was, after all, just a western, which was a genre that had not been in favor for some time. But every year there comes a time in early August when all the summer blockbusters have detonated and the movie world is ready for something serious, and good.

The reviews and audience response were superb. It was pretty much, "Welcome back, Clint!"—a mood that extended through the autumn, into awards season and, of course, right on to Oscar night. *Time* magazine film critic (and my longtime colleague) Richard Corliss summed up the film as Clint's meditation "on age, repute, courage, heroism—on all those burdens he has been carrying with such grace for decades. To anyone who appreciates what Clint Eastwood meant to the movies, old-fashioned is just another way of saying classic."

Clint was 62 when he won his Best Picture and Best Director Academy Awards for *Unforgiven*. It's an age when some men or women start (or finish) contemplating a run for President. It's certainly oldish for continuing to persevere as a movie star.

What did he have still to prove? He now possessed his industry's top prizes, plus a roomful of lesser hardware—with more, as it would turn out, piling up on the doorstep each year. He certainly would have been forgiven if he had decided to slip into something like semiretirement—a nice little role

occasionally, a directing job now and then, good-natured appearances at Hollywood's state occasions. Surely nobody was going to forget him anytime soon. He was—well, yes—an icon. He had become an icon. No question of that.

He could rest, and that would be fine.

But he couldn't rest. He could only keep on doing what he had long been doing, ever since he stumbled into *Rawhide:* show up for work, do your best, finish on time, go on to the next project.

Less than a year after *Unforgiven* he was acting

**HAVING SAT** on the script for *Unforgiven* (opposite) long enough, it was finally time to film the thing in 1992, and allow Will Munny to join No Name and Harry Callahan in the ongoing Legend of Clint. Never really a man of Hollywood—he purposely chose not to live there, once he was sufficiently established and could get out—he nevertheless enjoyed the Oscar ceremonies in 1993, as did his proud mother, Ruth.

(Wolfgang Petersen directing) in a first-class thriller, *In the Line of Fire*. He directed Kevin Costner (and himself) in *A Perfect World*, which was undervalued. *The Bridges of Madison County* brought Clint, as costar and director, into the realm of romance—and the orbit of Meryl Streep. The movie was based on a terrible best-seller but was redeemed by the honest playing of the leads. Streep is a shrewd observer of actors, and she noted in Clint a competitiveness that others had not observed—a competitiveness not with other actors but with his own past work, what he had accomplished, what he still wanted to do. She had worked with other actor-directors before and had noted them occasionally standing back from their scenes, watching as a director, not entirely in them as an actor. She called Clint on this once or twice, he owned to the fault, and theirs was among the happiest sets I've ever been on.

Clint wasn't on his unstoppable late-career roll just yet. *Absolute Power* featured Hackman as a notably cruel President; it was hardly a great film. *Midnight in the Garden of Good and Evil* was silly. *True Crime* was a newspaper yarn, more convincing than it probably had a right to be. *Space Cowboys* was a kind of geriatric lark, certainly as much fun to make as it was to watch.

If anything, Clint was working more than he ever had. Unnoticed, he was also reading more, and was about to make a decision about discernment. One thing that his many years had rewarded him with was invaluable experience in choosing and making movies. He now determined to lean on all of that experience, and he would never make another bad film, never make another picture that wasn't worth watching. He took pride in this, certainly.

Never said so, of course.

Clint Eastwood wouldn't.

**"I LIVE HERE,** not L.A.," Clint says of Carmel. "I'm there a lot, but this is home. When I was in the service, I came down to Carmel if I had half a day off, and I said, 'Boy, that's a place I'd like to live.' When I could, I did."

KEN REGAN/CAMERA 5

SIPA

KEN REGAN/CAMERA 5

**ON THE** opposite page, Clint smiles broadly at a press conference after his landslide election on April 8, 1986, as mayor of Carmel. Not just your everyday small-town civil servant, Eastwood tells reporters that none less than President Reagan just called to remind him that he, too, starred in a movie with a monkey (though never one with a talking mule). Presumably, Reagan offered congratulations as well. Eastwood says that he intends to begin implementing his ideas to improve Carmel immediately, but he later joked of his tenure in '86 and '87, "I phoned it in." (Everyone else says this is nonsense, that he worked very hard, that he simply won't accept praise without an instinctive deflection.) On this page, top row, he assumes his duties. Middle: He meets Pope John Paul II when the pontiff visits California. Right: The mayor and the law. It is doubtful that Clint is passing along to his Carmel cops any pearls of wisdom from the tao of Harry Callahan.

ARTHUR GRACE/ZUMA

KEN REGAN/CAMERA 5

**ON THE NEXT** four pages are photographs taken in 1995 for LIFE by Ken Regan on the set of *The Bridges of Madison County.* If you think it odd that Clint was directing and starring in the movie version of Robert Waller's melodramatic story of adultery, so did others at the time—in fact, it wasn't originally his project to direct but that of Bruce Beresford, who couldn't find a script, a farmhouse or even a bridge in rural Iowa that he liked. He finally quit, and Clint took over. He was adamantly against playing opposite a much younger woman, as the studio wanted, and insisted on casting a woman over 40. He called Streep, who hadn't enjoyed the novel, and got her to agree to read the screenplay. He FedExed a copy to Connecticut, she read it, called Clint and said, "I love it." He asked, "Will you do it?" She answered, "Yeah." Only weeks later the costars were just getting to know each other at the kickoff party at Wellman's Pub in Des Moines, when Clint said, "I hope you're not going to do a big accent thing." She had, of course, been perfecting an Italian lilt before heading out from the East Coast; she was immediately terrified and didn't sleep that night. In the event, Clint loved the accent, loved Streep's professionalism and performance. "She just transforms herself," he told LIFE. "Her gestures and her accent and everything." Streep said in turn: "He comes from so far afield, it was thrilling to see him do these emotional scenes. Unashamed. Unafraid. Weeping in front of the crew, then going to stand, bleary-eyed, behind the camera."

KEN REGAN/CAMERA 5

**IN THE MIDDLE** photograph above, real-life photographer Ken Regan talks things over with his friend Clint, who in *Bridges* will play a quiet, he-man photographer who rumbles into town and sweeps Streep off her feet. Clint needed no tips on how to woo a woman, but Regan, who has been a friend of Clint's for many years and has shot stills on many Eastwood sets, was able to coach him on how to hold a camera, how to hunch just so, how to pretend to be a photog in the field. (In fact, Clint borrowed Ken's cameras to use in the film.) Clint was stretching again in *Madison County,* playing the romantic lead, and he would stretch in a different direction with other friends of a certain age a few years later in the comedy *Space Cowboys* (on the following pages, from left, James Garner, Tommy Lee Jones, Donald Sutherland and Clint), another feature that he directed as well as starred in.

# THE MAN
## and the
# LEGEND

As Clint enjoys his eighties,
he is on top of his game
in many ways and places—on
the set, at home,
in the Hollywood pantheon.

The films of Clint's late years represent an unprecedented range of subject matter and style. Here is a man who has lived life fully, now reaching out in all directions for all kinds of meaning. Clint, in recent years, is even more completely on his own: Essentially, he can make what he wants to, how he wants to, with whom he wants to. Everyone will say yes. When she wrapped her role as FBI chief Hoover's controlling mother in Clint's recent *J. Edgar,* Dame Judi Dench was heard to murmur, "I've waited 75 years for this." Most of her contemporaries and many (much) younger actors share the sentiment, and hope to get to work with Clint before he finally unsaddles.

If he ever does.

Consider the run: *Mystic River,* marvelously complex and resonant, is the movie that began, in 2003, the string of late masterworks that persists to this day. Based on a Dennis Lehane novel, this tough story about the aftershocks of abuse and the parameters of "justice" won Oscars for Sean Penn and Tim Robbins, and is I think without parallel in the history of American film as a dark, enigmatic study of members of a closed society struggling to find light and meaning in a world where neither is readily available. *Million Dollar Baby* looked to be, ostensibly, a "boxing picture," and this was one where the studio was at first reluctant to commit. Clint didn't see a sports movie at all. To him, it was about a surrogate father, a boxing trainer played by Clint, finding his way to love in managing Hilary Swank to greatness and tragedy in a film that, to use the cliché, tears your heart out. It is small, intense, and it won Oscars for Swank, Morgan Freeman, and Clint (as director)—as well as for Best Picture. *Letters from Iwo Jima* (shot virtually simultaneously with the fine *Flags of Our Fathers*) undertook, with great daring, to examine World War II from the point of view of a Japanese general, played by Ken Watanabe. *Gran Torino* has Clint as a cranky old man who wants only to be left alone with his muscle car and his memories. He nevertheless is drawn into the lives of his neighbors, and there is violence and retribution that reminded some of Dirty Harry—though Clint never saw it that way, considering the new character both simpler and more complex than Harry. When you factor the low budget and hasty shooting schedule, *Torino* was, dollar for dollar, the most profitable hit of Clint's career. Faring less well with the audience was *J. Edgar.* But I wonder: Has there ever been a "biopic" less open about its subject's motives, less certain of what is moving the protagonist to his prodigious bureaucratic evil? Clint tells the story flatly, with Hoover an enigma to the end, and I think *J. Edgar* is some kind of a great movie, most particularly in its refusal to offer neat explanations.

"I keep working at this stage 'cause there's always new stories," Clint explains, "a new book or a new script that is interesting and worth telling. I'm always thinking outside the box. That keeps me out of a pattern of just saying 'Okay, westerns were successful for me, I'll just do westerns. Cop dramas were successful for me. I can just do cop dramas and call it a day—a paycheck, a few beers, a nice life.'

"But it wasn't enough. Personally it was not enough."

His voice, at this point takes on an unusual intensity. He talks about "straight strands"—looking for them in life, in his films. He backs off the intensity a moment later, and redefines it as "buzzing along." But that's clearly a Clint deflection; it's more than that, and he knows it, and he knows you know it.

His straight strand has brought him to seniority in a wonderful life, with a wonderful wife, a host of devoted children, a career that continues with unparalled success, an enviable golf handicap and a future his many admirers can only wonder at and happily anticipate.

What's next, Clint Eastwood?

**NO MATTER** where Clint turns, he confronts his storied past. Here, in Las Vegas on October 5, 2004, his wife, Dina, plays the new Fistful of Dollars slot machine. Eastwood has a marvelous sense of humor; almost everything he says has a little fun about it, a bit of teasing—teasing of his guests, his family or, most often, himself. His reply to the often asked question about whether he is at all bothered by the 35-year age difference in his marriage: "If she dies, she dies."

**WE ASKED** in our book's introduction: What makes an icon? The laurels certainly help. Among the highest in this country is to be cited as a Kennedy Center honoree—only five individuals each year, for lifetime achievement in the arts—and above, clockwise from top left, we have the class of 2000 at the State Department Gala: opera tenor Plácido Domingo, actress Angela Lansbury, Clint, rock 'n' roller Chuck Berry and dancer Mikhail Baryshnikov. At left, Clint receives the coveted Directors Guild Award in 2005, presented by his friend Steven Spielberg. Their association constitutes a mutual admiration society: When Spielberg produced his anthology TV series *Amazing Stories,* he asked Eastwood to direct an episode; and when Clint was wrestling with how to approach *The Bridges of Madison County,* he enjoyed nightly think-tank phone calls with his pal Steven. Opposite, top: In 2006 in Sacramento, two action heroes take the stage as Governor Arnold Schwarzenegger inducts Clint into the California Hall of Fame for his lasting contribution to the state, nation and world. Bottom: On May 11, 2007, in Los Angeles, University of Southern California graduating student Peter Akmetov holds his daughter Nicole as he is congratulated by Clint during the USC School of Cinematic Arts commencement ceremony. This day, the veteran moviemaker from the Bay Area receives not only a doctorate from the university but the first-ever Honorary Alumni Award from the film school. The honors, in the years to follow, just keep coming. And it is worth noting, Clint keeps showing up, politely and gratefully, always smiling.

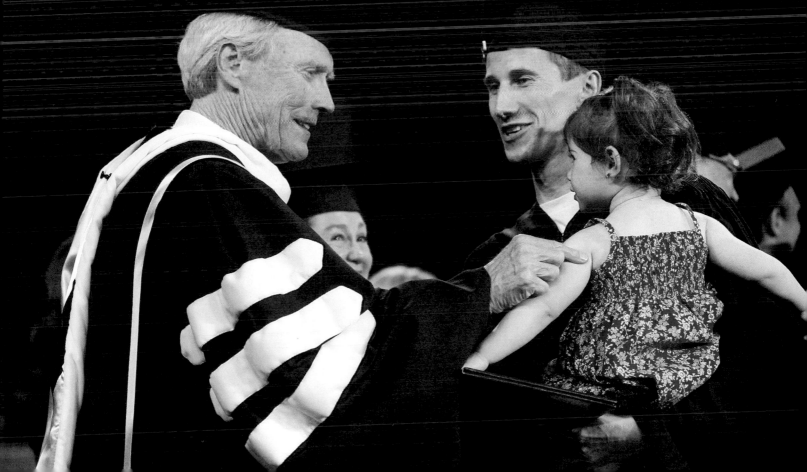

**DINA RUIZ,** a Salinas television news anchor, first interviewed Clint Eastwood in 1993. They subsequently dated and married on March 31, 1996, when Clint unveiled a surprise wedding ceremony at a golf course in Las Vegas. In December of that year, Clint became a father for the seventh time when daughter Morgan was born. At right, top, is a good chunk of the Eastwood clan at a 2002 movie premiere, including, from left, Kathryn, 14; Clint; Morgan, 5; Dina; Francesca, 9; Scott, 14; and the actress Frances Fisher. Clint and Frances lived together from 1990 until early 1995 and remain friendly today. Clint and Dina have been married more than 15 years now and have forged an impossibly idyllic life in Carmel, a life centered around family and their extraordinary Mission Ranch property. Clint recalls: "Back in 1951 I used to go to the bar down at Mission Ranch, and it was nice, just a dive with music and a dance floor. And then eventually it fell into disrepair, and so . . ." And so in 1987 Clint bought the expansive ranch that overlooks Point Lobos and threw a vault of money at it. Importantly, the bar they call the Small Barn "is just the same as it was in '51." There's music nightly, and Clint sometimes hangs out there with friends. Other parts of the sprawling Eastwood Carmel holdings include the family house and the extraordinary Tehama golf course, with horseback riding adjacent. (Fun fact: Clint is allergic to horses. Yes, Clint Eastwood has an allergy to horses.) For all the undeniable luxury of Clint's existence as he has constructed it, his wife insists he—and they—do not live an opulent lifestyle. "He'll be there getting groceries," she recently told the Web site Celebuzz. "Or go to the feed store, because he'll be buying the hay and the animal food. He's the most grounded guy I ever met . . . We drive beat up cars. We shop at Marshalls."

FRANK TRAPPER/CORBIS

KELLI ULDALL/CARMEL MAGAZINE (2)

**CLINT SPOKE** earlier in our pages about the rhythm he values in life, speculating that this is why he enjoys things like music and golf—"they have rhythm in common." The man himself prefers a smooth rhythm. He seeks it in his golf swing, at the keyboard, on the movie set. He might have made a movie about bop idol Charlie Parker, but Clint's piano playing owes more to Erroll Garner than it does to Bud Powell, and if you get him going on the very smooth singer Johnny Hartman, whose music Clint boosted in *The Bridges of Madison County,* you're in for quite a disquisition. It is suggested to him during one of these conversations that a lot of the rhythms of his life are flowing quite smoothly these days. "That's true," he allows. He is reminded of a nifty metaphor he used with Steve Kroft in the *60 Minutes* interview. He told Kroft that he was on the back nine of life and was playing a lot better, maybe under par on the recent holes, after a rugged front nine with a lot of mistakes. Had he figured that out before being interviewed? "I don't think I thought about it beforehand," he says. "But you never know what you might've thought about before, really." With things going well for him in his seniority, Clint seems to imply that, just perhaps, he is taking things a bit easier—and then he quickly corrects the impression. "I don't really like to hurry anymore with the career," he says. "I don't have to." Does that mean that the career means less to him than it used to? "Oh no," he says. "I'm just not hurrying things anymore. And as I mentioned, there are other things I'm enjoying." It's irresistible to ask, when considering Clint Eastwood in full: Does he feel lucky? He surely does. He has always been lucky when luck was needed: The guy in the hall asks him to do *Rawhide;* The Man with No Name falls out of the sky and lands on his desk; Paul Newman is turned off by *Dirty Harry* and passes. But Clint has been as good and as hardworking as he has been lucky. He didn't make *Josey Wales* or *Unforgiven* by any kind of accident, or *Mystic River* or *Million Dollar Baby* or *Gran Torino.* He didn't marry Dina by accident, and he doesn't have a passel of kids devoted to Dad by accident. Yes, his front nine had their divots—some mediocre movies, some vicious critics, some rocky relationships—but he has found himself, on what golfers call "the home holes," standing in the middle of a perfect fairway, looking at a welcoming green, no sand in sight. He takes a breath before attempting his next shot, confident because so many of the recent shots have landed so nicely. Who wouldn't feel lucky?

**THERE'S NO**
mistaking whose golf
cap this is, as the motto,
in Latin, translates:
Make my day.

(DANA GALLAGHER)